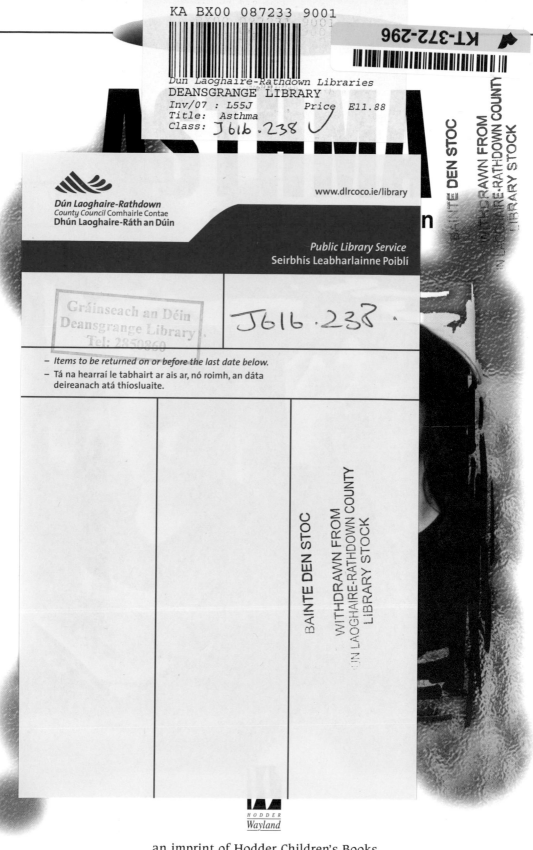

HODDER
Wayland

an imprint of Hodder Children's Books

© 2002 White-Thomson Publishing Ltd

White-Thomson Publishing Ltd,
2-3 St Andrew's Place, Lewes,
East Sussex BN7 1UP

Published in Great Britain in 2002 by Hodder Wayland, an imprint of Hodder Children's Books. This paperback edition published in 2003.

This book was produced for White-Thomson Publishing Ltd by Ruth Nason.

Design: Carole Binding
Picture research: Glass Onion Pictures

The right of Sarah Lennard-Brown to be identified as the author of this work has been asserted by her in accordance with the Copyright, Designs and Patents Act 1988.

British Library Cataloguing in Publication Data
Lennard-Brown, Sarah
  Asthma. - (Health Issues)
  1. Asthma - Juvenile literature
  I. Title II. Nason, Ruth
  616.2'38

ISBN 0 7502 4558 1

Printed in Hong Kong by Wing King Tong

Hodder Children's Books
A division of Hodder Headline Limited
338 Euston Road, London NW1 3BH

Acknowledgements

The author and publishers thank the following for their permission to reproduce photographs and illustrations: Martyn Chillmaid: page 53; Corbis Images: pages 7 (George Lepp), 18 (Hulton-Deutsch Collection), 24 (Dave Bartruff), 25 (William James Warren), 41 (Robert Stevens), 51 (Rodney Hyett; Elizabeth Whiting & Associates), 59 (Guy Motil); Mark Edwards/Still Pictures: page 31; Angela Hampton Family Life Picture Library: pages 6, 13, 14t, 23, 34, 40, 42, 43, 44, 47; Mediscan: cover and pages 1 and 12; National Asthma Campaign: page 26-7; Photofusion: pages 16 (David Montford), 30 (Clarissa Leahy), 32 (Don Gray); Popperfoto/Reuters: pages 36, 37, 49, 56; Science Photo Library: pages 4 (Cordelia Molloy), 5 (Martin Bond), 10t (Dr P. Marazzi), 14b (James King-Holmes), 17 (BSIP, Laurent/Fred), 20 (Dr Jeremy Burgess), 21 (Carl Schmidt-Luchs), 22 (BSIP Edwige), 27 (Carlos Goldin), 33 (Eye of Science), 38 (Damien Lovegrove), 39 (Hattie Young), 46 (Saturn Stills), 54 (Geoff Tompkinson), 58 (Mark Clarke). Artwork and photographs on pages 8, 9, 15, 35 and 50 are from the Wayland Picture Library.

Note: Photographs illustrating the case studies in this book were posed by models.

Contents

Introduction
Who has asthma?   **4**

1 Asthma, airways and breathing
The effects of the disease   **6**

2 Asthma triggers
From allergies to stress to thunderstorms   **16**

3 Asthma and the environment
Where triggers occur   **26**

4 Treating asthma
Medication and therapies   **38**

5 Living with asthma
Be a good manager!   **50**

Glossary   **60**

Resources   **62**

Index   **63**

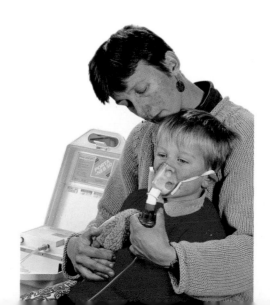

Introduction
Who has asthma?

Asthma is a disease that affects your airways. When someone has an asthma attack, their airways become inflamed and narrow. This means that they may experience whistling or wheezing as they try to get air into and out of their lungs. They may also find it hard to get *enough* air into their lungs, and this can make them feel tight across the chest, breathless, frightened and tired. The Global Initiative for Asthma estimates that approximately 150 million people worldwide suffer from asthma.

In Chapter 1 we explore exactly what happens to the airways during an asthma attack and how asthma is diagnosed. There are many things that can trigger an asthma attack and we look at these in Chapter 2. An important point about asthma is that it is 'reversible'. The airways respond to a trigger, such as animal hair or stress, by becoming inflamed. This response reverses when the trigger is removed or when treatment is given.

It seems that the higher the standard of living of the country in which you live, the more likely you are to suffer from asthma. The highest incidence of asthma is found in Australia and New Zealand. In 1998, 28.2 per cent of Australian 13-14 year-olds had been diagnosed with asthma at some time during their lives. This compares to 20.7 per cent of 13-14 year-olds in the UK, 16.5 per cent in the USA, 12.6 per cent in France and 1.6 per cent in Albania (International Study of Asthma and Allergies in Childhood, 1998). The UK has the highest rate of asthma in Europe. The lowest rates are found in poorer countries such as Albania, China and India.

Asthma attack
When a person has an asthma attack, the airways in their lungs become narrower, making it difficult to breathe.

There is much debate about the reasons for these differences in the numbers of people affected by asthma. In Chapter 3 we examine some of the possible reasons, including the effect of increasing wealth and improvements in housing on the environments in which we live; changes in air quality; pollution; and smoking. There is also debate about whether increasing levels of asthma are related to modern standards of cleanliness and freedom from infection. Your level of exposure to asthma triggers at work and at home is one factor determining whether you are at risk from the disease. Your genetic make-up also plays a part.

Counting the costs

Asthma is a serious problem. If not properly treated and controlled, it can be fatal. In 1997, 1,584 people died from asthma in the UK alone. More than one third of these were people below the age of 65. The National Asthma Campaign estimates that the cost of treating asthma to the National Health Service in Britain was approximately £709 million in 1997. Asthma also has a substantial cost in time lost at work and school, not to mention the distress of asthma itself.

The treatments that are available for asthma are described in Chapter 4, and Chapter 5 looks in depth at the issues associated with living with asthma, keeping in control of asthma symptoms and living life to the full.

Relief
A reliever inhaler contains a medicine to help the user breathe more easily during an asthma attack.

1 Asthma, airways and breathing
The effects of the disease

Asthma is a disease that affects your airways and makes it difficult to breathe. Breathing is important; if we stop breathing, we stop living. In order to understand the impact of asthma on the lives of people who suffer from it, we need to understand how and why we breathe, and what happens to a person's airways when they have an asthma attack.

Why breathe?

When you breathe, you take air from the environment around you, through your airways, into your lungs. As your lungs fill with air, an amazing reaction happens. Oxygen (a gas present in the air) is absorbed into your bloodstream, and carbon dioxide (a waste product from your body) is removed from your bloodstream and expelled into the environment as you breathe out.

You need to absorb oxygen in order for your body to function. Oxygen is vital to life. It is carried to every part of your body by your bloodstream. Every cell of your body needs a continuous supply of oxygen in order to make the energy that it needs to live. The oxygen reacts with the nutrients such as proteins, carbohydrates and fats that you get from the food you eat, to produce energy. Without oxygen, cells are unable to produce energy and they quickly stop functioning and die.

Feel-good factor
The clean air on a cliff top helps us to feel full of energy.

When each individual cell uses oxygen to create energy, it also creates waste products. This is rather like the engine of a car, using petrol to create the energy that it needs to move but also creating waste exhaust fumes. One of the main waste products made by your cells is a gas called carbon dioxide. This gas is dissolved into your bloodstream and taken back to your lungs, from which it is expelled when you breathe out.

How you breathe

When you breathe in air from your environment, you use the muscles around your rib cage and diaphragm to suck the air into your lungs. This is called inhaling or inspiration. You also use these muscles to push air out of your lungs (exhaling or expiration). The part of your body involved in breathing is called the respiratory tract.

The upper respiratory tract (or upper airway) includes your mouth, nose, pharynx and larynx. Your mouth and nose serve as a passageway for the air, filtering, warming and moistening it on its way to the lungs. Your nose also protects your lungs from unwanted irritants and large particles in the air, with a sneezing reflex.

Burn up
Just like us, cars need fuel to produce the energy to move, and burning fuel produces exhaust waste.

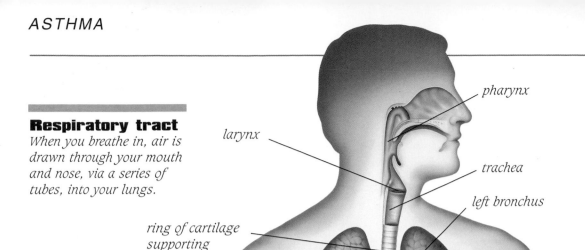

Respiratory tract
*When you breathe in, air is
drawn through your mouth
and nose, via a series of
tubes, into your lungs.*

pharynx

larynx

trachea

left bronchus

ring of cartilage
supporting
trachea

bronchiole

heart

left lung

diaphragm

Your pharynx is the place where the tube from the mouth
and nose divides so that food can travel on to your
stomach and only air goes into your lungs. When you eat
or drink, your pharynx automatically seals off the airway
to your lungs in order to stop food or fluid entering the
lungs. This reflex is very important; it prevents you
drowning every time you have a drink of water, for example.

Your larynx is where you produce the sound of your voice.
Both the larynx and the pharynx protect the lungs with a
cough reflex if they are irritated. This prevents foreign
bodies (like dust and small objects such as peanuts)
entering your lungs and also clears mucus (a clear fluid)
produced by the lungs.

The lower respiratory tract is made up of the trachea, the
left and right bronchi (lower airways), bronchioles and
alveoli. Your trachea acts as a passageway extending from

your larynx and dividing into two bronchi (left and right), which take the air deep into your lungs. Each bronchus divides and divides again into smaller and smaller bronchioles, and then even smaller alveolar ducts, which take the air directly to the alveoli, the part of your lungs where the crucial action takes place.

Alveoli are minute sacs of lung tissue surrounded by tiny blood vessels called capillaries. The walls of both the alveoli and the capillaries are very thin. This means that oxygen can pass through the sides of the alveoli into the capillaries, where it is captured and transported around your body by blood cells. At the same time, carbon dioxide passes out of your blood, through the walls of the capillaries and into the alveoli. The waste carbon dioxide is removed from your lungs when you breathe out (expiration).

The clever way in which the lungs are formed means that the air you breathe in reaches a large surface of alveoli. The surface area of the alveoli in your lungs is estimated to be between 30 and 40 times the size of your body surface. This means that nearly every particle of gas or dust contained in the air you breathe, that is not filtered out by your upper airway, will come into direct contact with your lower airways and the alveolar surface of your lungs.

Alveoli

Oxygen from the air passes through the walls of the alveoli into the capillaries.

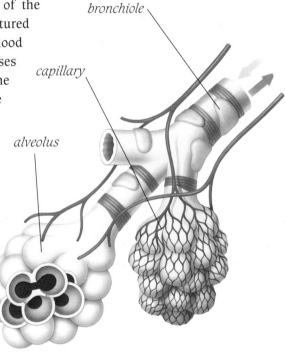

bronchiole

capillary

alveolus

One result of this is that your lungs are very efficient at extracting the oxygen your body needs from the air you breathe in and getting rid of the waste carbon dioxide gas from your bloodstream. However, another result is that, if your airways are sensitive to any of the particles in the air you are breathing, a large expanse of lung can be affected. This is what happens when you have asthma.

ow asthma affects your airways and breathing

People with asthma have very sensitive airways. The way your lungs react when you have asthma is very similar to the way your skin reacts when you are stung by a nettle. The area that has touched the stinging nettle becomes red and swollen. Similarly, if something irritates the airways of a person with asthma, the airways become red and swollen and this may make the person's chest feel tight.

When airways become red and swollen, they get narrower. This makes it more difficult for air to pass through the airways into the alveoli and out again, and so the person becomes breathless – that is, they breathe faster to get enough oxygen into their body. It takes a lot of effort to get air in and out through narrow airways and the force needed can result in a whistling noise, usually called a wheeze.

Inflamed areas also produce fluid – just as, when you touch a stinging nettle, you sometimes get small, fluid-filled blisters. This is part of the body's self-protection system, the immune response (see page 19). Irritated airways produce lots of fluid (mucus) to try to flush out the irritant. This results in the asthma sufferer coughing as they try to clear the mucus from their lungs in order to be able to breathe properly.

Nettle rash
The inflammation produced by a nettle sting is similar to the inflammation in your lungs when you have asthma.

Inflamed airways
A normal airway (right) compared to an inflamed airway of someone with asthma (far right).

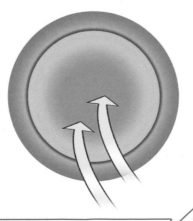

At this point, the asthma sufferer hits another problem: it is very difficult to cough up mucus properly if your airways are narrow and inflamed. This means that the sufferer is caught between trying to cough up mucus and trying to breathe in and out to get enough oxygen into their system. It can be frightening to experience an asthma attack and the person often feels very scared and anxious. The fear and anxiety can also cause breathlessness and so make the airways close up even more. Asthma attacks can be dangerous; sometimes they can be fatal. They need prompt medical attention.

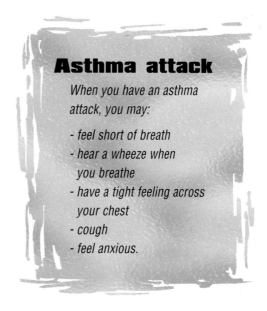

Asthma attack

When you have an asthma attack, you may:

- feel short of breath
- hear a wheeze when you breathe
- have a tight feeling across your chest
- cough
- feel anxious.

Asthma attacks vary in how severe they are and how often they occur. Some people with asthma only experience them occasionally, perhaps when they have a virus infection such as a cold. Others experience these symptoms more regularly, such as after exercise or during the night. A few people with very severe asthma feel like this most of the time. However, one of the main features of asthma as a disease is that it is reversible: the inflammation can be soothed, without leaving permanent damage. Sometimes the airway inflammation subsides on its own, but often properly prescribed medicine is required to soothe the airways and open them up, making it easier to breathe.

'I sometimes get asthma when I have a cold. I have these coughing fits where I can't get anything up but I can't stop coughing. It keeps me awake at night.'
(Jake, student)

The long-term outlook for people with well-controlled asthma is good, but for people who have severe, poorly controlled asthma there can be long-term problems. These can include lack of growth, due to repeated chest infections and the energy demands of breathing with asthma.

What to do when someone has an asthma attack

Usually people know that they have asthma and carry medicine in the form of inhalers with them (see page 39). When they have an asthma attack, they know to take a couple of puffs of their reliever inhaler. This is usually enough to get their asthma back under control. Sometimes, however, it is not enough and urgent action is required. If someone appears to be having an asthma attack but does not have their inhalers with them, or has never had an attack before, the best course of action is to sit them down, keep them calm and call for an ambulance.

Keeping help at hand
People who have asthma usually carry inhalers, which help them to breathe more easily during an asthma attack.

Practical advice

The National Asthma Campaign advises everyone with asthma to discuss with their doctor or practice nurse what they should do if they have an asthma attack. The recommended steps are:

1. *Take your reliever straight away, as directed by your doctor, preferably using a spacer.*
2. *Keep calm and try to relax as much as your breathing will let you. Sit down – don't lie down. Rest your hands on your knees to support yourself. Try to slow your breathing down as this will make you less exhausted.*
3. *Wait 5-10 minutes.*
4. *If the symptoms disappear, you should be able to go back to whatever you were doing.*
5. *If the reliever has no effect, call your doctor or an ambulance.*
6. *Keep taking your reliever inhaler every few minutes until the ambulance arrives.*
7. *Take your steroid tablets if your doctor has written them into your self-management plan.*
8. *Do not be afraid of causing a fuss, even at night.*

Diagnosing asthma

When doctors try to find out what is causing your health problems, they use several techniques. They start by talking to you to find out your symptoms. Symptoms are the unusual things that are happening to you, which sent you to the doctor in the first place; for example, a cough that won't go away. If you have asthma, you may well have a cough and a feeling of tightness around your chest. You may also have a wheeze and be short of breath. Some people have all these symptoms; others may have just one or two. Other important information includes how often these symptoms occur, how long they last and how severe they are.

Your doctor may also ask about the timing of symptoms and if your environment affects them; for example, do you feel worse at night or when it's foggy or when you exercise? You may be asked about your medical history; you are more likely to have asthma if you already have an allergy-related illness such as eczema or hay fever. Do any other members of your family have asthma? There is some evidence that a tendency to develop asthma may be genetically inherited so, if other members of your family have asthma, there is a chance you may develop it too.

Diagnosis
In order to diagnose your problem doctors listen and ask questions.

Your doctor may also want to listen to your chest, using a stethoscope. This enables them to hear clearly what is going on inside your body. If you have asthma, your doctor may be able to hear wheezing in your airways when you breathe in and out. They will also be able to hear if you have a chest infection.

Other tests that help your doctor decide whether you have asthma include:

⚫ Peak flow tests: These measure your peak expiratory flow rate (PEFR), which is how much air you can blow out in a short amount of time – and so they give a good idea of how narrow your airways are. Your doctor may ask you to do peak flow tests at home, night and morning, for several weeks. Doing so will show up any variations in your lung function over time, and give an indication of whether your airways are getting sensitive and narrow overnight or during the day.

Measure your airways
Peak flow meters measure how well your lungs are functioning.

⚫ Spirometry: This may be performed by your family doctor or at a hospital respiratory clinic. It is a more sophisticated version of a peak flow test. You are asked to breathe out as hard and fast as you can, for as long as you can, into a spirometry machine.

Spirometry
A spirometry test may be carried out at a hospital clinic.

⚫ Bronchoprovocation test: This test is much less common and is usually performed in hospital. First you have a spirometry test; then you breathe in a small amount of a substance that provokes an asthma attack and another spirometry test is done to see if your airways have narrowed.

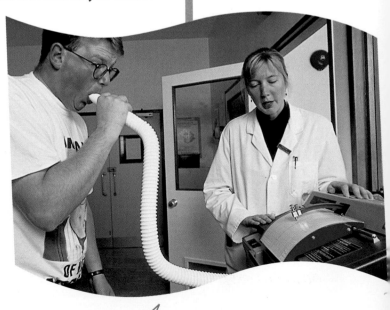

Blood tests: These are to see if you produce a specific antibody called immunoglobulin E (IgE) whilst you are experiencing asthma. It may indicate that your asthma is caused by an allergy.

The tests used to diagnose asthma look at what happens to your airways during an asthma attack and try to find out what causes the changes that occur. The causes of asthma are difficult to pin down, but many things can provoke an asthma attack and these are called triggers. In Chapter 2, we will look at what the triggers are and how they affect the airways of people with asthma.

Learning from experience

I was about five when I was diagnosed with asthma. I used to cough a lot and not be able to stop. It would wake me up at night and could be quite scary. Then the doctor gave me a reliever inhaler that helped and I took another inhaler, a preventer, every day to calm down my airways and stop them getting narrow. That stopped the worst of it, but it still gets bad sometimes – particularly in the autumn when the mould spores are produced.

Bad attacks are very frightening. I've only had to go to hospital once and I was so glad to get there. Not being able to breathe is a horrible experience, and then when your inhalers don't seem to work … But as soon as the ambulance arrived and they gave me some oxygen I felt better, and the hospital gave me a nebulizer, which really helped. I only had to stay overnight, but I needed some steroid tablets to get over that attack. Knowing what to do is the trick. These days I see an asthma nurse regularly and we have a plan of what to do if my asthma gets bad. So far so good. (Kelly, college student)

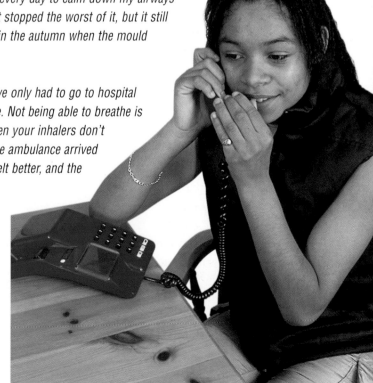

2 Asthma triggers
From allergies to stress to thunderstorms

Asthma triggers

Allergies to:
- animal hair and feathers
- house dust mites
- moulds
- pollen

Viruses

Exercise

Stress and emotion

Some medicines

Cigarette smoke

Air pollutants

Hormones

Weather conditions

Asthma is a complex disease that is still not fully understood. Asthma symptoms are the result of your airways becoming inflamed and narrow. Anything that irritates your airways, making them inflamed and narrow and effectively starting an asthma attack, is called a trigger.

Allergy is one of the most common asthma triggers but there are many others. Other triggers include viruses, exercise, cigarette smoke and chemicals.

Trouble with dogs

My asthma's caused by dogs. Every time I get anywhere near a dog I start wheezing. It's really embarrassing. My mates think it's a good laugh and every time they see a dog they start pushing me towards it, 'Oh look Mark it's your best friend' – that sort of thing. It wasn't funny even the first time. The puffer (reliever inhaler) sorts the wheezing out, and the doc's sending me to an allergy clinic; she thinks they may be able to do something to help, desensitization or something. I hope so. It's not the dogs that are the problem as much as my mates – I wish the doctor could desensitize me to them.
(Mark, aged 15)

Allergies

An allergy occurs when your immune system (the system your body uses to protect you from infection) mistakes a harmless substance for a dangerous one (see page 19). Usually your immune system is very good at telling the difference between harmless substances and viruses, bacteria and parasites that could be very harmful to the body.

Allergies range in severity. Allergies to insect stings and some foods can be fatal (this is very rare). At the opposite extreme are minor conditions such as hay fever, which causes discomfort and aggravation during the pollen season.

Hay fever
Sneezing and watering eyes are two symptoms of hay fever. Antihistamine tablets usually help.

The relationship between allergies and asthma is complex. Not all asthma is caused by allergies and not everyone who suffers from allergies has asthma. You are most likely to have asthma caused by an allergy if your asthma started in childhood. For people who develop asthma in adulthood, only about half the cases are related to an allergic reaction.

Your chances of developing an allergy depend on your genes and your environment. Some people inherit a tendency to develop allergic reactions, through their genes. You may find that one member of a family has hay fever, another eczema and another asthma. Sometimes one individual may be unlucky enough to have more than one condition. This tendency to develop allergies is called 'atopy', and seems to be related to slight changes in the gene responsible for the production of an antibody called immunoglobulin E (IgE). Antibodies are protein molecules produced by your immune system, and they destroy bacteria, viruses and parasites. Inheriting this changed gene does not mean that you will definitely develop an allergy, since other factors also play a big part, but it does mean that you are more likely to develop an allergy.

The number of people suffering from allergies is growing, particularly in richer societies. One American study in 1999 found that 38 per cent of Americans were affected by allergy. It is thought that this is due to changes in the environment in developed countries. One issue is that of increasing cleanliness. Some people think that our immune systems may need to be exposed to regular small doses of dirt and disease in order to give them a work-out and keep them healthy. In rich countries, people now tend to live in super-clean environments and children are less likely than in the past to play outside, grubbing around in the dirt; therefore, their immune systems do not get the challenges they need to develop properly. Under-developed immune systems are thought to be more likely to make the mistakes that cause allergies. Some researchers are even working on microbe (dirt) vaccines that would give our immune systems a work-out whilst not making us ill.

Healthy dirt?

Some researchers feel we need to come into contact with some dirt and bacteria for our immune systems to develop properly.

You are more likely to develop an allergy if you are exposed to allergy-causing substances, especially in the first few months of life. It has been found that babies born in late spring or early summer are more prone to develop an allergy to pollen and so suffer from hay fever or asthma. There is also some evidence that you are more likely to develop an allergy to pet hair if you have a pet when you are young.

Antibodies and allergy

For an allergy to develop, the immune system must become sensitive to the substance that causes the allergy (often called an allergen). Here's how it happens. Antibodies patrol your bloodstream looking for substances that could cause you harm. One of these antibodies makes a mistake and fastens to a harmless substance. The antibody then attaches itself to special cells called mast cells. Your immune system is now sensitive to the allergen.

Once you have been sensitized, your body will respond quickly the next time it detects the allergen in your bloodstream. Your body releases large amounts of IgE into your system, and your mast cells, which are now primed and ready for action, release large amounts of a chemical called histamine into your bloodstream in order to repel what is now considered a dangerous invader. It is histamine that causes the symptoms of allergy. It makes your blood vessels (the tubes carrying your blood around your body) expand and leak fluid, and it can also make your airways narrow. A rash (often called hives) may develop and you may feel your heart beat faster.

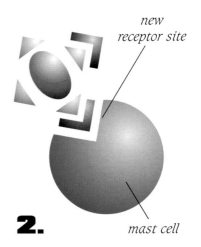

pollen grain
antibody
1.

new receptor site
mast cell
2.

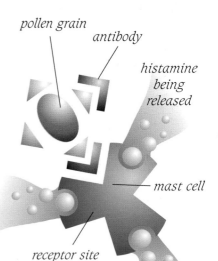

pollen grain
antibody
histamine being released
mast cell
receptor site
3.

The mechanism of allergies

1. *An antibody fastens to a pollen grain, which it has mistaken for a dangerous invader.*
2. *The antibody takes the pollen to a mast cell which 'remembers' it by creating a unique receptor site.*
3. *When another pollen grain enters, the mast cell recognizes it and produces excess histamine, to fight it. This causes inflammation.*

Pollen
Many people have a mild allergic reaction to pollen.

How strongly you react to the allergen depends on how much histamine is released by your mast cells. Some allergies caused by things such as bee stings can result in lots of histamine being released and can be fatal. This is often referred to as anaphylaxis. Allergies to substances like pollen, house dust mites, pet hair and moulds are usually less severe and cause conditions such as asthma, hay fever, perennial rhinitis and eczema.

Anaphylaxis

Anaphylaxis is the name given to the most severe form of allergic reaction. It is very rare and usually only a problem for people who are allergic to foods (such as peanuts and other nuts, shellfish and seafood), bee or wasp stings, or latex (found in products such as rubber gloves and balloons). It is not a problem usually associated with asthma.

In susceptible people, anaphylaxis usually happens within twenty minutes of being exposed to the allergy-causing substance. They may find that their skin starts itching and a red rash may erupt over their body. Their lips may tingle and swell; they may become hoarse and start to wheeze. They get a feeling of tightness across the chest and they may feel short of breath and giddy. They may also feel confused and anxious. Sometimes they lose consciousness and, if not treated promptly, anaphylaxis can be fatal.

If someone does have a severe allergic reaction, it is important to get them to hospital very quickly. Often people who have this sort of severe allergy carry an injection of adrenalin with them. Adrenalin reverses the symptoms of anaphylaxis very quickly.

Allergies that trigger asthma

Asthma triggered by allergies is usually caused by four main common substances:

Animal hair and feathers

Substances that can cause allergies are shed from the feathers, fur, urine, droppings and saliva of birds and animals, including rats, mice, cats and dogs.

'I have an allergy to cat hair. The cat doesn't have to be there. If I go into a house where there is a cat I start to wheeze and have to take a puff of my inhaler.'
(Shuheb, aged 22)

House dust mites

The droppings of house dust mites are responsible for approximately 80 per cent of cases of allergic asthma. They can also cause perennial rhinitis and hay fever.

Fungi

Fungi are the fruiting bodies of mould spores. (See page 31.)

Mould spores

These can be found both indoors and out. Moulds thrive in warm damp conditions. Their spores can provoke an allergic reaction in susceptible people and this can be a problem in late summer and autumn.

Pollen

Pollen is a common allergen and can cause problems in spring and early summer when plants and trees produce pollen in order to reproduce.

Often people talk about food allergies that trigger asthma but these are very rare. Some people feel that they are sensitive to certain foods, which make their asthma symptoms worse. Foods commonly named for this are dairy products, fish, wheat, nuts and foods containing yeast. This is not a food allergy but a food intolerance. Some food additives and colourings have been found to trigger asthma symptoms but this is uncommon.

'Late summer is the worst time. I'm allergic to moulds. So no walking through the autumn woods, unless I take my inhaler with me.' (Jonathan, aged 44)

Allergy tests

Tests used to diagnose allergy-related asthma include blood tests and skin prick tests.

Blood tests measure the amount of the antibody IgE in your bloodstream while your symptoms of asthma are worst. Occasionally, doctors ask for a blood reaction test, where an allergen is added to a sample of your blood whilst it is under a microscope. The sample is then watched to see if it reacts to the allergen.

Skin prick tests involve inserting tiny amounts of common allergens into the upper layers of your skin through tiny pricks. The test areas are then observed after a few days to see if they have become inflamed. If a test area has become inflamed, this shows that you are allergic to the allergen inserted there. These tests can be very useful in identifying what you are allergic to, but sometimes the results can be misleading as an allergen that produces a skin reaction may not necessarily produce asthma, and vice versa.

Many people claim to be able to work out what substances you are allergic to by methods such as analysing a sample of your hair, or testing your muscle tone. Beware of these kinds of tests, as there is no evidence that they are able to diagnose allergies. The only reliable tests for allergy at the present time are those performed at medically recognized allergy clinics.

Testing
Skin prick tests are used to diagnose allergies.

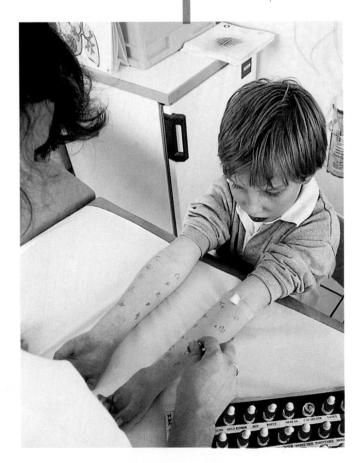

Other triggers

Not all asthma is triggered by an allergy. Other asthma triggers include virus infections, exercise, stress and emotion, medicines, cigarette smoke, air pollutants, some household and industrial chemicals, weather conditions and hormones.

Virus infections

Virus infections are very common asthma triggers. Approximately 80 per cent of people with asthma find that virus infections make their asthma symptoms worse. Virus infections, including colds and flu, cause inflammation in your airways, and this can trigger asthma symptoms. Often these symptoms continue long after the actual infection has gone away.

Take it easy
Exercise can trigger asthma symptoms.

Exercise

Some people with asthma have permanently inflamed and irritated airways so, when they start to exercise and need to take in more oxygen to meet their body's needs, they have to work even harder – and the effort involved can trigger an asthma attack.

Stress and emotion

The link between our feelings and the way our bodies react is very complicated. The fact that some people's asthma is triggered by emotion does not mean that it is all in the mind. It is not only worry and anxiety that can trigger an asthma attack. Some people's asthma is triggered by laughing or excitement.

'I get wheezy when I'm choked up. I sit there in weepy films, being all butch and not crying, and wheezing like crazy. It's a bit of a give-away.'
(Tod, aged 20)

Medicines

Some medicines such as aspirin, non-steroidal anti-inflammatory drugs and beta-blockers have been found to trigger asthma.

Cigarette smoke

Cigarette smoke is a very common trigger. It contains a potent cocktail of chemicals that are very efficient at irritating your airways. As with viruses, approximately 80 per cent of all people with asthma have their symptoms triggered by cigarette smoke.

Air pollutants

These include traffic fumes, fumes from gas cookers, central heating boilers and bottled gas heaters, and smoke from fires and barbecues. Many people are concerned that air pollution causes breathing problems like asthma. However, while air pollution has been found to make asthma symptoms worse in people who already have the disease, there is no evidence that air pollution *causes* asthma to develop in people who are not genetically susceptible to it. From the increase of people with asthma worldwide, it does appear that large numbers are genetically susceptible.

A smoky bar

I started to get asthma when I worked in a bar. It began slowly. I noticed my chest felt a bit tight after work at night. Then it got worse. I'd be up half the night coughing. I got really tired. Then it started while I was at work. I just seized up one night, coughing and all. I was taken to hospital and they said I had an asthma attack. It seems my chest got irritated by all the cigarette smoke in the bar. I had to change my job, but it's all right now.
(Rhianne, waitress, aged 23)

Household and industrial chemicals

These include chemicals such as paints, perfumes, solvents, the ink in marker pens, spray cleaning products and polishes. People working with petroleum-based chemicals, paints and solvents are prone to develop occupational asthma (see page 31).

'I was worried my asthma would get worse when I was pregnant, but it didn't. It was miles better. One of the better things about being pregnant.'
(Esme, aged 32)

Hormones

For women with asthma, changes in hormone levels can have an effect. For example, some women find that they are more prone to develop asthma symptoms at certain times during their menstrual cycle. Often women with asthma find that their symptoms get either better or worse during pregnancy or menopause.

Weather conditions

Many people find that their asthma is triggered by breathing cold air. Other weather conditions can also trigger an attack, including changes in temperature, fog, damp, wind, thunderstorms and hot still days with poor air quality.

In the next chapter we will look at asthma triggers in more detail and examine the impact of our modern environment and lifestyle on people with asthma.

Thunderstorm

Weather conditions such as thunderstorms can trigger asthma attacks.

3 Asthma and the environment
Where triggers occur

Asthma occurs when a genetically susceptible person meets factors in their environment that trigger an asthma attack. People all over the world have asthma, but there are some places where larger proportions of the population suffer from it. The reasons for this are not yet fully understood, but it seems that the more 'Westernized' a society becomes, the higher the number of people with asthma.

Australia and New Zealand have the highest incidence of childhood asthma. The World Health Organization and the National Heart, Lung, and Blood Institute carried out a study called 'Global Strategy for Asthma' (1995). It found that 45 per cent of children in Australia and New Zealand had positive allergy tests and about 20-27 per cent of children in Australia and approximately 17 per cent of children in New Zealand had asthma.

Campaigners
Many people who have asthma join an organization like the National Asthma Campaign, and take part in activities to raise awareness of asthma.

World Asthma Day

Asthma is increasingly a global problem. With an estimated 150 million people suffering from asthma worldwide, many national asthma organizations have combined their resources to start World Asthma Day. On this day each year, usually in May, events are staged around the world to raise awareness of asthma and put asthma on the international agenda.

Why are these figures so high? One suggestion is that there is a high degree of sensitivity to allergies in the populations of these countries, combined with air pollution from cigarettes, cars and industrial pollution.

Other areas with a high incidence of asthma include the USA, Canada, South America and the UK. Lower incidences of childhood asthma were found in Asia, Africa and continental Europe. One of the most interesting findings of the Global Strategy for Asthma study was that you are more likely to get asthma if you live in an urban area. For example, you are more likely to have asthma if you live in a polluted urban area of Sweden than if you live in the Swedish countryside. In Chile, school children in urban polluted areas have a much higher incidence of asthma than those in the countryside.

The urban environment

There is a strong link between air pollution and asthma. The Global Strategy for Asthma also looked at asthma rates in two polluted German cities: Munich, which has a high degree of pollution from car exhausts, and Leipzig, which has a high level of industrial pollution. They found that asthma was more

Car exhausts
Pollution from car exhausts has been linked to high levels of asthma.

common in Munich (cars), while Leipzig had a higher incidence of bronchitis (a different lung disease). In Japan, pollution from diesel engines has been linked to an increase in people suffering from allergies to a common Japanese plant called *Cryptomeria japonica*. It is thought that chemicals present in air pollution affect the lung lining, making it more sensitive. Therefore smaller amounts of allergen or any other trigger are needed to provoke an asthma attack.

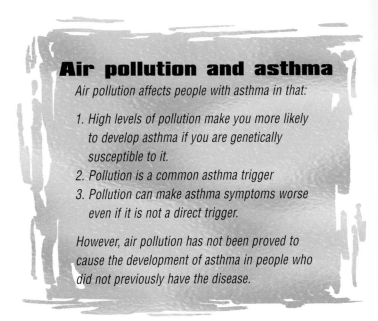

Air pollution and asthma

Air pollution affects people with asthma in that:

1. High levels of pollution make you more likely to develop asthma if you are genetically susceptible to it.
2. Pollution is a common asthma trigger
3. Pollution can make asthma symptoms worse even if it is not a direct trigger.

However, air pollution has not been proved to cause the development of asthma in people who did not previously have the disease.

Air pollution affects many countries around the world. Some cities have such a problem with poor air quality due to car exhaust fumes that they limit the cars entering the city. In Paris, France, during the summer months, the authorities regularly restrict the number of cars allowed

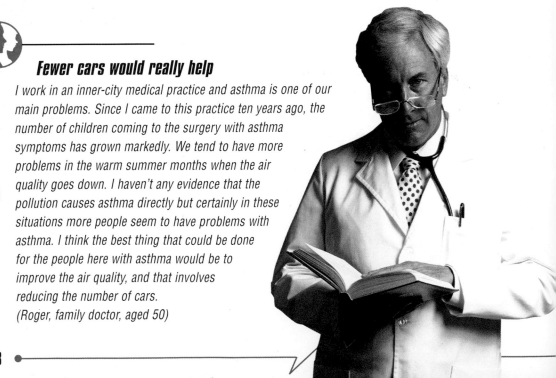

Fewer cars would really help

I work in an inner-city medical practice and asthma is one of our main problems. Since I came to this practice ten years ago, the number of children coming to the surgery with asthma symptoms has grown markedly. We tend to have more problems in the warm summer months when the air quality goes down. I haven't any evidence that the pollution causes asthma directly but certainly in these situations more people seem to have problems with asthma. I think the best thing that could be done for the people here with asthma would be to improve the air quality, and that involves reducing the number of cars.
(Roger, family doctor, aged 50)

into the city. The Committee on the Medical Effects of Air Pollutants estimates that in Britain up to 14,000 deaths each year can be attributed to air pollution and this number includes deaths from asthma.

The natural world: pollen time

Pollen is a powerful allergen and is linked to several allergic illnesses including asthma. There are many different varieties of pollen. Some people are sensitive to just one variety and so will experience more asthma symptoms when that particular pollen is in the air. Others are sensitive to a variety of pollens and their symptoms will be more long-lasting. There is concern that new genetic engineering techniques are changing pollen grains in subtle ways. Little is known about the impact this will have on allergies and asthma.

Pollen grains

Some pollens are more likely to provoke an allergic response than others. Grass pollens are particularly bad.

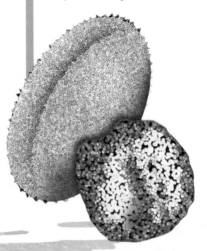

Oil-seed rape

Oil-seed rape is grown in the northern hemisphere for its oil, which is used in cooking, and as a food crop for animals. It has also been developed for use as a fuel oil as an alternative to petrol. The number of farms growing oil-seed rape has steadily increased as more industrial uses are found for the oil.

The pollen is said to be so irritating that it makes even horses sneeze. However, in 2000, the Committee on the Medical Effects of Air Pollutants (UK) found that oil-seed rape was rarely the cause of allergies. They did find that the pollen grains could be irritating to the eyes, nose and lungs, without causing an allergy, and this would explain why some people experience a worsening of asthma symptoms when the crop is in flower.

Breast-feeding

Breast-feeding has been found to reduce the likelihood of a child developing an allergic disease (including asthma). This is especially so if breast-feeding is continued for the first year of life. Breast milk gives a baby some immunity as well as nutrients from its mother, and this may help the baby's own immune system to develop properly and protect the baby from various diseases. Breast milk is also much easier for a baby to digest and, unlike cow's milk, does not contain substances that can cause sensitivity.

It has been found that children born during the pollen season are more likely to develop asthma. When babies are born, their immune systems are immature and they are vulnerable to infection. Because of this, they are also likely to develop allergies if they are genetically susceptible. Recent research has highlighted the importance of reducing the number of allergens to which babies are exposed, in order to reduce the likelihood of them developing allergic diseases.

Pollen Timetable

Spring	Trees
Late spring to mid-summer	Grasses
Mid-summer to early autumn	Weed pollen

Moulds – outdoors and indoors

Mould spores can trigger an allergic reaction in some people. This can cause perennial rhinitis or asthma. Mould spores can be found in warm or cool moist places, outdoors or inside. Moulds are part of the natural ecosystem in woodland, where they help to break down plant and animal material into vital nutrients needed by other plants. Mould spores are like seeds from a plant: they are mould's reproductive system. They are released into the air usually during late summer and autumn, a time when you often see their fruiting bodies – fungi and mushrooms.

Our well-insulated, warm homes are prime breeding grounds for moulds. They thrive on windows prone to condensation, in damp areas around sinks, in bathrooms and in damp walls and roofs. Spores from these sorts of mould can be released at any time of the year.

Changes in the weather

Cold air is a trigger for many asthmatics and contributes to an increase in asthma attacks during the winter. Cold air can be a shock for airways used to warm, centrally heated homes, and this can irritate the airway lining and trigger asthma.

Sudden changes in air temperature can trigger an asthma attack, as can damp and fog. Some people with asthma find that their symptoms become worse on hot still summer days as the air pollution rapidly gets worse and any pollen in the air is not blown away. Others find that their symptoms get worse at the onset of a thunderstorm or when atmospheric pressure is particularly high.

The workplace

Modern working environments often bring people into contact with potential triggers. These can cause asthma to develop in those who are susceptible to asthma but have never had any symptoms before. Asthma caused by triggers in the workplace is called occupational asthma.

Latex
Latex is a potential asthma trigger, so workers in a factory producing latex gloves wear a protective head covering.

Some occupations involve working with more potential triggers than others. The main occupational asthma triggers include:

- Latex. This occurs particularly in medical occupations, which often involve wearing latex gloves.
- Isocyanates. These are chemicals often used in adhesives, foams, paints and plastics.
- Fumes from soldering and welding: often used in the electronics industry.
- Some floor cleaners. They contain organochemicals, which can be irritating.
- Dust, especially from grains (including flour), wood dust (especially hard woods and western red cedar), latex dust.

Protection
Wearing a mask helps to protect these workers from fumes and dust.

Where there's smoke ...

Cigarette smoke is a powerful trigger for up to 80 per cent of asthma sufferers as it contains a strong mixture of irritating chemicals. People with asthma do not have to smoke a cigarette themselves for their asthma to be triggered; merely smelling someone else's cigarette smoke can be enough. This can have far-reaching consequences if you have asthma, especially if you live in a country where a large number of people smoke. Someone severely affected by asthma can become a prisoner in their own home, unable to go out for fear of breathing cigarette smoke and having a severe asthma attack.

'Cigarette smoke's my trigger. One whiff and that's it: I'm coughing and wheezing. Should be banned.'
(Tony, car factory foreman)

The situation has improved over the last few years in some countries. In the USA, the UK and many northern European countries there have been attempts to reduce the amount of smoking in public places. In the UK, smoking has now been banned from public transport and cinemas, some restaurants and many other public places.

Sharing their home with someone who smokes can be hazardous for people with asthma. Babies born into a smoker's family are far more likely to develop asthma than babies born into non-smoking families. They are even more likely to develop asthma, as well as other problems, if their mothers smoke whilst pregnant.

House dust mite
This coloured electron micrograph shows a house dust mite among skin scales in household dust.

Asthma triggers at home
House dust mites

Worldwide, house dust mites are the most common cause of allergic asthma. These microscopic creatures love our modern standards of living; they flourish in warm, humid conditions and live on the skin cells that we shed every day. It is not the mites themselves that are potent allergens, but their droppings. The mites live in our warm, unventilated homes, in bedding and soft furnishings, curtains, carpets, cushions, soft toys, and anywhere dusty. They are present in their millions, even in the cleanest homes.

The effect of living with a high concentration of house dust mites was demonstrated some years ago in Papua New Guinea, where there was a sudden rise in the number of children with asthma. When the situation was investigated, it was found that the rise in childhood asthma happened soon after the population started to use woollen blankets. The environment in Papua New Guinea is warm and humid, conditions loved by

Beware ...
House dust mites commonly live in:
- *mattresses*
- *duvets*
- *quilts*
- *blankets*
- *sheets*
- *pillows*
- *bed spreads*
- *carpets*
- *rugs*
- *curtains*
- *cushions*
- *fabric-covered chairs and sofas*
- *soft toys*
- *dust anywhere.*

house dust mites, and the blankets provided an ideal breeding ground for them. As the concentration of house dust mites in the home increased, so did the incidence of childhood asthma.

Pets

It is possible to develop allergies to the hair, skin scales (dander), saliva, urine and faeces of animals and birds. Any home with a pet will be full of these microscopic particles, especially in soft furnishings where they get trapped and are difficult to dislodge. Research in the USA, of which the results were published in June 2001, found that more than 330,000 cases of asthma in children could be directly related to having a pet in the household.

Natural gas

Natural gas is a popular fuel for heating and cooking, especially in the UK. The gas itself is not a problem, but when it is burnt during cooking, it increases the level of nitrogen dioxide in the air in the home. Although this is not a trigger itself, it can make an asthma sufferer more sensitive to other triggers.

Cleaners – and an over-clean environment

Many common household cleaners contain chemicals called volatile organic compounds, which can trigger asthma. These chemicals are made from oil and petroleum and can irritate your airways. Other products containing these chemicals include air fresheners, paints, glues, varnishes, and some aerosol sprays.

An issue related to the use of chemicals in our homes is the production of an over-clean environment. Over-clean environments are not triggers in themselves, but there is

Cats
Some people are allergic to cats. They notice the symptoms of their allergy when they visit a cat-owner's home, whether the cat is in the room or not.

Air freshener

The doctor told me I'd got asthma when I was 60. I didn't think anyone could start asthma that old. He asked me if anything made it worse. Well, I couldn't think of a thing. Eventually I worked out it was the new air freshener I used in the downstairs lavatory. They didn't tell you about that on the television advert. Anyway, it was easily solved – I changed brands.
(Pamela, housewife)

increasing concern that lack of contact with dirt when we are children may mean that our immune systems do not mature enough to work properly. There is growing scientific evidence to support the idea that, if our immune systems do not get enough practice, then they are more likely to make mistakes and react against harmless allergens as if they were dangerous viruses, bacteria or parasites. (See also page 18.)

Medicines that can trigger asthma

Some medicines can trigger asthma symptoms in some people. These drugs are important tools for fighting some difficult diseases and only rarely cause asthma attacks. However, the reactions can be severe and therefore people with asthma should always double-check with their doctor before taking the medicines. Medicines that have been found to trigger asthma in susceptible people include:

- Aspirin: (acetyl-salicylic acid). This drug can provoke a severe and potentially life-threatening asthma attack in approximately 3 per cent of people with asthma. This can even happen to people who have never reacted badly to aspirin before. Therefore it is strongly recommended that people with asthma avoid all products containing aspirin.

- Other non steroidal anti-inflammatory drugs, such as ibuprofen, indomethacin and diclofenac sodium.
- Beta-blockers – taken as pills to treat high blood pressure and as eye drops for glaucoma, for example, betaxolol.

Why virus infections trigger asthma

Approximately 80 per cent of people with asthma find that virus infections make their asthma symptoms worse. Virus infections including colds and flu are usually spread by coughing and sneezing. This distributes live viruses into the air, which are then breathed in by anyone unlucky enough to be nearby.

'My son's had asthma since he was six months old. It's usually worse in the winter, especially if he gets a cold.'
(Janet, insurance clerk)

The viruses settle in your airways and multiply, causing irritation and making you sneeze and cough so that you send more viruses out to infect other people. Your immune system notices that it has an unwelcome visitor (or a few thousand) and sets to work to eradicate them before they can do major harm. Your body's first response to a viral invader is to start the process of inflammation. This makes your airways red and

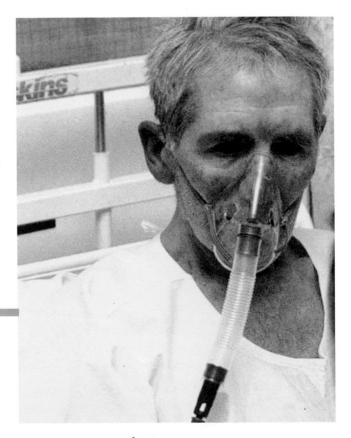

Colds and flu
Virus infections such as coughs and colds can trigger asthma. A vulnerable elderly person may need to be treated in hospital.

swollen. Your airways produce lots of mucus in order to try to clear the virus out, and lots of antibodies swarm to the area in order to remove any virus that is left. Unfortunately, these are the very things that produce asthma symptoms in susceptible people.

If asthma sufferers get a virus, their airways may swell and narrow, producing the tell-tale wheeze, shortness of breath and tight chest. Once the symptoms of asthma have started, they often continue for a long time after the infection has been eliminated.

Asthma on the increase

The tendency to develop allergies and asthma is to some extent inherited through our genes, but the environment in which we live plays a large part in determining whether we go on to develop asthma. The number of people suffering from asthma has increased rapidly over the last few decades. The factors that are currently thought to be the most likely causes of this increase, working either separately or together, are:

- increases in the number of women smoking whilst pregnant
- increases in the amount of air pollution from cars and industry
- decreasing exposure to childhood illnesses and infections
- less well ventilated homes – leading to a higher build-up of allergens and pollutants
- increase in soft furnishings in affluent homes – leading to larger numbers of house dust mites.

(from Dr M. Partridge, 'Asthma: a global problem', *Asthma News*, July 1997)

Pollution

This cyclist wears a heavy-duty anti-pollution mask, to prevent him breathing in exhaust fumes from traffic in the city. Increased air pollution is thought to be one likely cause of the increase in asthma.

4 Treating asthma
Medication and therapies

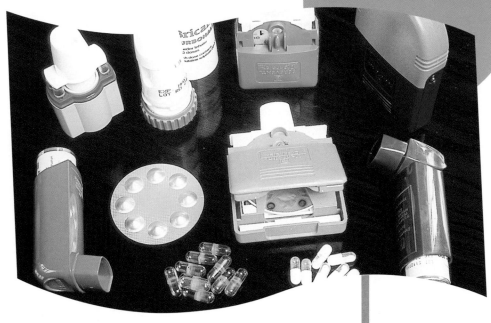

Treating asthma needs to be a two-pronged attack: you must (1) reduce your exposure to asthma triggers and (2) take the medication prescribed by your doctor regularly.

There are many excellent treatments for asthma. If you have asthma, your doctor will work out which is best for you as an individual. People with asthma often need more than one type of treatment. Your doctor and asthma nurse will help you put together a treatment plan that is right for you. Your asthma and the amount of medication you are taking need to be monitored to make sure that you take the least amount of medication necessary to control your symptoms. If your symptoms get worse, then the medication will be increased. if they improve, the medication will be decreased.

Medicines for asthma are usually divided into two types: relievers and preventers. Relievers act quickly to help you to breathe more easily. Preventers are more long-

Medication
Common treatments for asthma include various types of inhalers and tablets.

'Once you get used to the puffers it just becomes part of life – something you do like cleaning your teeth.'
(Esme, student)

Relievers

There are several types of reliever:

- *Salbutamol – fast-acting reliever (inhaler)*
- *Terbutaline – fast-acting reliever (inhaler)*
- *Ipratropium bromide – can take up to 45 minutes to take effect (inhaler)*
- *Oxitropium – long-lasting reliever (inhaler)*
- *Salmeterol – long-lasting reliever (inhaler)*
- *Eformoterol – long-lasting reliever (inhaler)*
- *Xanthine – long-lasting reliever (tablets)*

term. They work by reducing the inflammation and sensitivity of your airways to triggers, and so prevent asthma symptoms occurring.

Relievers

Relievers are usually prescribed as inhalers. Inhalers are a form of medicine that you breathe directly into your airways so that it starts work immediately at the site of the problem. Relievers work by making the muscles around the inflamed, narrow airways relax. This means that the airways can open further, making it easier to breathe.

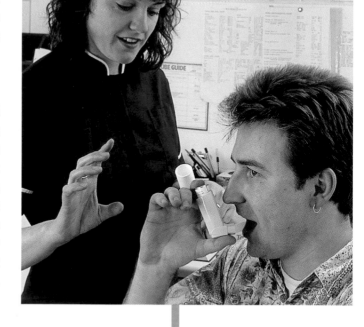

There are few side effects associated with taking reliever inhalers. Some people experience a fast heartbeat and trembling after taking Salbutamol, but this usually gets better quickly. Xanthine tablets occasionally make people feel a little sick.

Asthma nurse

Some nurses specialize in helping people with asthma. They monitor treatment and give health education and advice.

Preventers

There are several types of preventer:

- Beclomethasone – steroid (inhaler)
- Budesonide – steroid (inhaler)
- Fluticasone – steroid (inhaler)
- Sodium cromoglycate – mast cell stabilizer (inhaler)
- Sodium nedocromil – mast cell stabilizer (inhaler)
- Zafirlukast, montelukast – antileukotrines (tablets)
- Cetirizine, loratadine - antihistamines (tablets)

Preventers

Preventers are also usually given in the form of inhalers. Preventers work by soothing the lining of the airways. They reduce inflammation and make the airways less sensitive to triggers. This means that, when you take preventers correctly, you are less likely to experience a severe asthma attack. For preventers to work properly you have to take them every day (usually twice a day), even if you feel well. They also take up to 14 days to start working.

Steroid inhalers

Inhaled steroids are a very effective form of treatment for asthma. Each dose (or puff from the inhaler) contains a tiny dose of cortico steroid. Cortico steroids are not the same as the steroid drugs sometimes abused by bodybuilders and sportsmen. Cortico steroids are a medicine that reduces inflammation. They mimic chemicals naturally produced in our bodies that soothe inflammation and irritation. Inhaling this medicine has the advantage of taking it straight to the inflamed airways that need soothing. This means that only tiny amounts of the medicine are needed and that there are very few side effects.

Spinhaler
Inhaling through a spin-haler causes a fan to spin very fast, dispensing a dry powder medicine into your lungs.

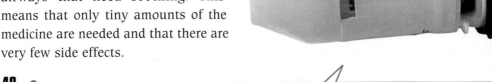

Side effects from steroid inhalers are mainly limited to a sore mouth. Occasionally, people have been known to develop a condition called thrush in their mouth whilst taking inhaled steroids. This problem can be reduced or avoided by rinsing your mouth or cleaning your teeth after using the inhaler. It can also be avoided by using a device called a spacer when you inhale the medicine.

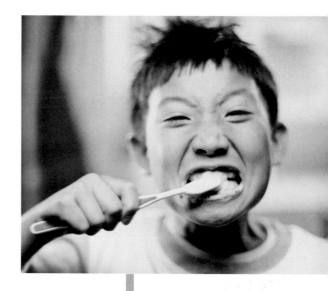

Other side effects such as osteoporosis, growth suppression, bruising and eye problems are much less common. These side effects only become a problem for people who are taking high doses of inhaled steroids for a very long time. Osteoporosis, bruising and eye problems may be a problem for older men and women, and growth suppression can affect children on high doses, although asthma itself can cause children not to grow as fast as children without asthma (see page 11). Children who are prescribed high-strength steroids have their growth closely monitored by their family doctor, in order to check that this does not become a problem.

Brush up!
Cleaning your teeth after using inhaled steroids can prevent you getting a sore mouth.

Mast cell stabilizers

These medicines work on mast cells, which are part of the immune system. When this system mistakes a harmless substance for a harmful one, an allergy is started. Once sensitized, mast cells react to the presence of allergens (substances that cause allergies) by releasing the chemical histamine into your bloodstream. This chemical causes the symptoms of allergy. Mast cell stabilizer medicines calm down these cells and stop them being so active. This reduces the level of inflammation in your airways and makes them less sensitive to any allergens you breathe in. There are no side effects associated with these medicines.

'The medicine's good. I couldn't sleep a whole night for coughing. But now it's sorted.' (Imran, mechanic)

Antileukotrines

Leukotrines are chemicals found in the muscles around your airways and in the lining of your lungs. People with asthma seem to produce a lot of these chemicals and this is thought to contribute to the amount of inflammation in their airways. The leukotrines affect the muscles around the airways, making them irritable (twitchy) and causing them to grow larger.

These things can combine to make your airways narrower and so it is harder to breathe in and out. Antileukotrines stop the build-up of these chemicals in the muscles and lining of the airways and so reduce the amount of inflammation and stop the muscle in the airways being so 'twitchy'; it is then easier to breathe. Antileukotrines are new medicines but, so far, there do not seem to be any major side effects associated with taking them.

Inhalers

Medicine for asthma is usually breathed straight into the airways. This is so that the smallest dose necessary can be used and the medicine goes straight to where it is needed. Doctors often prescribe the medicine in the form of an inhaler. Inhalers are either dry powder or aerosol (often called puffers or metered dose inhalers). There is a knack to using an inhaler and if you have asthma you will probably spend some time with a nurse, learning how to use this treatment. Using an inhaler can be difficult if you are having a bad asthma attack, as you have to breathe the

Using an inhaler

1. Breathe out as far as you can.
2. Press the end of the inhaler in order to release the medicine at the same time as you breathe in slowly and deeply.
3. Hold your breath for 10 seconds to ensure the medicine has enough time to reach deep into your airways before it is breathed out.

'It was a bit tricky getting the hang of using the puffer. But once I'd cracked it, it was easy – like riding a bike.'
(Stan, retired painter)

medicine in deeply and hold your breath for a few seconds so that the medicine can reach your lower airway. It is much easier to use an inhaler with a spacer.

Breathe easy
Spacers make it much easier to use an inhaler.

Spacers

Spacers are large plastic containers with a hole at one end, to fit the inhaler, and a mouthpiece at the other. Using an inhaler with a spacer ensures that the whole dose of medicine enters your lungs. It also reduces the risk of side effects from inhaled steroids, as less of the steroid is swallowed and absorbed into the body. The idea is that you press the inhaler to release a dose of medicine into the spacer and then you can breathe this in more slowly. There are many types of spacer and each one needs a slightly different technique.

Nebulizers

Nebulizers are machines that pump air through a mixture of medicine and saline (salty water) in order to create a fine mist. These machines are mostly used to give high doses of reliever medicine in hospital. Nebulizers can be noisy and cumbersome and, since spacers have become much more efficient, they are not often used at home.

Thanks to steroid tablets

To my mind, steroids are wonderful! The first time I took them I'd been ill with a chest infection and asthma for ages. It just wasn't getting better. I felt terrible. Then the doctor prescribed me steroid tablets. I was nervous of taking them – you hear so many horror stories. But in my case their effect was miraculous! My lungs cleared and I had more energy within two days. I wouldn't like to take them for too long, mind you. (Julie, debt counsellor, aged 36)

Steroid tablets

Occasionally people with asthma find that their symptoms get worse. At these times, their doctors may prescribe steroid tablets. These are a much stronger dose than a steroid inhaler and they are very effective at reducing airway inflammation. Steroid tablets are usually taken first thing in the morning. This is because, if they are taken later, they can make it difficult to sleep at night. Usually the steroid tablets need to be taken only for a short period of time (3 to 14 days) and side effects are not a problem, although the tablets can make you less resistant to the chickenpox virus. You should contact your doctor if you are taking steroids and then are exposed to chickenpox.

If steroids are taken for a long time, then there is a risk of side effects. These include growth retardation (mainly a problem for children who are still growing), developing a round (moon) face, weight gain (due to an increase in appetite), bruising and osteoporosis. People who are on steroids for long or short periods of time need to carry a steroid card with them. This is so that if they have an accident, the doctor treating them will know that they are on steroids.

Chickenpox
Taking steroid tablets can make you vulnerable to chickenpox.

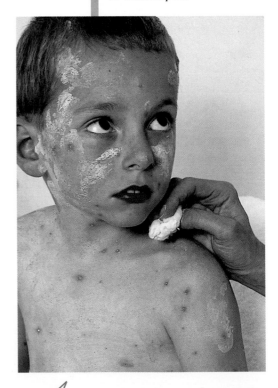

Antibiotics

A chest infection may be more dangerous for people with asthma than it is for others. If they develop a chest infection, people with asthma may need treatment with antibiotics. Antibiotics are very effective at treating infections caused by bacteria. There are many forms of antibiotic and each has its own requirements for how to take it and its own side effects. In general, the side effects from antibiotics are minor but can include feeling sick, upset stomach, and diarrhoea. (Diarrhoea following antibiotics should be reported to your doctor.) Occasionally you can have an allergic reaction to an antibiotic, particularly the penicillin range of antibiotics. You may develop an itchy rash and sometimes swelling around your face and lips. If this happens, you need to stop taking the antibiotic and contact your doctor for advice.

'I often get chest infections in the autumn when my asthma is bad. The doctor gives me antibiotics, which help.'
(Alex, farmworker)

Allergy treatments

If you have asthma that is caused by an allergy, then it may be possible to have a desensitization treatment. Desensitization treatment involves attending an allergy clinic where you will be given a series of injections over several months.

The treatment begins with skin prick testing to confirm what you are allergic to (the allergen). This is followed by a series of tiny injections containing minute amounts of the allergen. These injections may continue for a long time. It varies depending on the individual but can be from several months to five years. The aim of the injections is to retrain your immune system not to react to the allergen. It is important to try to avoid the allergen while you are having the desensitization injections.

Desensitization treatment can be very effective at reducing the severity of allergy-induced asthma and if you react well to the treatment, improvement in symptoms can last for several years after finishing the injection course. There is a small possibility of having an anaphylactic reaction to desensitization injections. This is rare but can be severe. Therefore, desensitization treatments should always be performed by a competent medical practitioner with emergency equipment available. In practice, this usually means that it is best to have the treatment in a hospital allergy clinic.

Antihistamine

Histamines are chemicals produced by your immune system, which cause inflammation. Antihistamines are medicines that stop the inflammation process. They are sometimes used with other treatments for asthma caused by allergies to things such as fur or pollen. Antihistamines can make you feel tired and drowsy.

Emergency and hospital treatment

Occasionally people with asthma have a severe asthma attack, which does not respond to the reliever medicine that they keep with them. This is more likely if they have a virus or chest infection.

Hospital treatment

It was really frightening taking our son Dan to hospital. He's so small and he couldn't get his breath. You know it all runs through your head, 'Am I making a fuss? Is he going to die?' I'd hate to get there and find it was nothing, but I couldn't take the risk. As it turned out, it was fine. They said I'd done the right thing. They gave Dan a nebulizer and I stayed with him all the time. It really helped. He stayed in overnight and came home with some medicine to take for a while. I feel a bit more confident about knowing when to ask for help now. (Rene, mother of Dan)

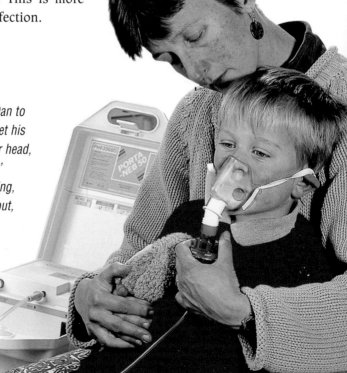

If an asthma attack does not improve after a dose of reliever medicine, then contact your doctor or call an ambulance and keep taking your reliever medicine every few minutes until the ambulance arrives. Don't be afraid of causing a fuss, even at night.

In hospital, the doctor will assess you and may give you some oxygen to help your breathing. You may well also be given a nebulizer with a high dose of reliever medication. This will help improve your breathing. If you have a chest infection, you may be given intravenous antibiotics and steroid tablets to reduce the inflammation in your airways. If you are admitted to hospital with an asthma attack, you may need to stay overnight or a few days until your asthma is under control again.

Complementary therapies

No complementary therapy can cure asthma, but some can help you manage it better and sometimes reduce your symptoms. If you want to try a complementary therapy, do not stop taking your prescribed medicine and do let your doctor know. This is important, as some complementary medicines can be harmful for people with asthma. Complementary treatments for asthma can be divided into four sections: exercise, relaxation, hands-on therapies and medicines.

Exercise

Exercise-based therapies such as yoga, Pilates, t'ai chi and martial arts can all have a beneficial effect on asthma symptoms. This is because they increase your general fitness level and they all involve breathing exercises, which can help you stay in control during an asthma attack. Another potential benefit from these exercise

T'ai chi
Exercises such as t'ai chi can help you to control your breathing.

therapies is that they involve learning to relax. Knowing how to keep calm and relaxed when an asthma attack occurs can help you prevent the attack from becoming severe.

Relaxation

Relaxation therapies such as visualization and meditation can help you learn to relax. This will certainly help if your asthma is triggered by stress and can also help you to cope with asthma attacks, which can be very frightening and are made worse by fear and tension.

'Meditation really helps. When I get an attack I try to do the relaxation thing and focus on my breathing.'
(Sheila, beautician)

Hands-on therapy

Acupuncture involves the insertion of very thin needles at points on your body, based on Chinese theories of natural energy paths. Some research into the benefit of acupuncture for people with asthma has shown that it can be helpful in the short term. Acupuncture does not normally produce side effects. However, you should make sure that you are seeing a properly qualified practitioner who is using sterile acupuncture needles.

Massage can be beneficial for people with asthma in that it imparts a feeling of relaxation and well-being. As we have seen, relaxation can help reduce asthma symptoms by reducing stress.

Complementary medicines

These include herbal medicine, Chinese herbal medicine and homeopathy. Some herbal medicines have been shown to help reduce asthma symptoms. Herbal medicines that may be helpful include ginko biloba, tylophora asthmatica, coleus forskholii and saiboku-to. However, there is little conclusive evidence in this area. Some herbal medicines can be harmful for people with asthma and you should always ask your doctor's advice before taking a herbal preparation.

'I tried some alternative stuff, but it did nothing for me, waste of money.'
(Aidan, computer operator)

Some products from bees, particularly Royal Jelly and propolis, which are commonly sold as medicinal products, can be very dangerous for people with asthma. They can provoke a severe allergic reaction. It is wise to avoid any products containing Royal Jelly and propolis if you have asthma or allergies.

Homoeopathic treatments involve a detailed assessment of your particular problems and character and then treatment with tablets containing a very tiny amount of a substance that would produce similar symptoms if taken in large doses. Homeopathy can be helpful if you know what your triggers are. Some research has shown that homeopathy can be helpful for some people with asthma – particularly a form of homeopathic treatment called homeopathic immunotherapy. However, more research is needed to prove the value of this treatment.

The second component of successfully managing asthma involves reducing your exposure to triggers. In Chapter 5 we will investigate how you can do this, as well as issues to do with living with asthma.

The benefits of yoga

I think yoga's got a lot to offer someone suffering from asthma. It's all about being more aware of your body, aligning and stretching, improving flexibility and stamina, also relaxation and breathing. Every movement flows from your breath. You learn to control your breathing and to breathe effectively. As an asthma sufferer myself, I think yoga has helped me be more in control.
(Aisha, yoga teacher)

Living with asthma
Be a good manager!

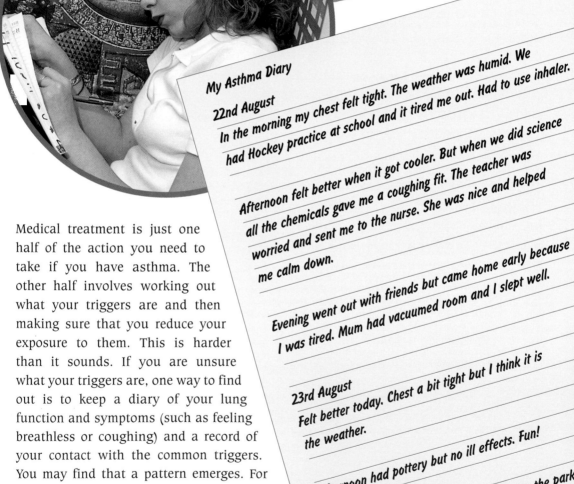

Medical treatment is just one half of the action you need to take if you have asthma. The other half involves working out what your triggers are and then making sure that you reduce your exposure to them. This is harder than it sounds. If you are unsure what your triggers are, one way to find out is to keep a diary of your lung function and symptoms (such as feeling breathless or coughing) and a record of your contact with the common triggers. You may find that a pattern emerges. For example, your symptoms may be worse in the morning and improve during the day. This might indicate that you are sensitive to something in your bedroom, perhaps house dust mites. You could then take action to reduce

My Asthma Diary

22nd August

In the morning my chest felt tight. The weather was humid. We had Hockey practice at school and it tired me out. Had to use inhaler.

Afternoon felt better when it got cooler. But when we did science all the chemicals gave me a coughing fit. The teacher was worried and sent me to the nurse. She was nice and helped me calm down.

Evening went out with friends but came home early because I was tired. Mum had vacuumed room and I slept well.

23rd August

Felt better today. Chest a bit tight but I think it is the weather.

Afternoon had pottery but no ill effects. Fun!

Saw Sarah in evening and we walked to the park. It was clear and cool (in more ways than one because I saw Steve there!!)

your exposure to the suspected triggers and see if there is an improvement in your symptoms. Once you have worked out what your triggers are (and it may be more than one thing), you can take action to reduce the amount of contact you have with them.

Reducing triggers at home

Your home is a prime site for asthma triggers – especially house dust mite droppings. Eliminating house dust mites from your home is almost impossible, but there are several things you can do to reduce their numbers dramatically.

The mites live on the skin cells we shed every day. They like a warm, moist environment to live and breed in – and breed they do: there are millions of them in the average bed! House dust mites love bedrooms, which are warm and full of soft furnishings, bedding, carpets and cuddly toys in which the mites like to live. If you find that house dust mites are a trigger for you, then start your elimination campaign in your bedroom. Here are some useful tips for getting rid of dust mites:

- If you can afford it, replace old worn mattresses, pillows and duvets.
- Change your bedclothes regularly (weekly if possible) and wash the sheets at a high temperature.
- Consider buying house dust mite-proof covers for your mattress and pillows.
- Wash soft toys and then put them in a plastic bag in the freezer for a few hours. Cold temperatures kill dust mites.
- Cushions and pillows also benefit from a regular stay in the freezer (if you have one large enough).
- Vacuum using a vacuum cleaner with a special filter, and damp dust regularly. (Some people who are very sensitive to dust mites need to do this daily.)

At home
Making your home less attractive to house dust mites does not mean that you need to make it less stylish.

- Reduce the amount of soft furnishings in your home. Use blinds instead of curtains. Make sure any soft furnishings left are vacuumed and cleaned regularly.
- Replace carpets with hard flooring such as lino or wood.
- Make sure there is adequate ventilation. Open windows and air your home and bedding daily.

Smoking

Cigarette smoke is a trigger for 80 per cent of asthma sufferers. Anywhere that people smoke can be difficult for people with asthma. It is extremely unwise to smoke cigarettes if you have asthma. It is also unwise to live with anyone who smokes. Even if they never smoke in the house, the smell of smoke left on their clothes or in their hair can trigger an asthma attack in someone who is sensitive to it. If you have asthma, never allow people to smoke in the house and avoid going to places where people smoke.

Pollen

If your asthma is triggered by pollen, you will find that it is worse at certain times of the year. Pollen is very hard to avoid as it blows for many miles. Keeping windows and doors shut and staying inside as much as possible during the pollen season are practical things you can do to reduce your exposure.

Using vacuum cleaners with special filters and damp dusting daily during the pollen season can help too. If you are severely affected, it is possible to purchase high-powered air filters which can filter pollen from the air.

Some areas tend to have a higher pollen count (a measure of the amount of pollen in the air) than others; in general, the pollen count tends to be less on the coast, as there are sea breezes to blow the pollen away. Updates on the pollen count are published in most local newspapers and on television and radio, and these give you a guide as to when to take more precautions.

Domestic gas

If you cook using domestic gas, there will be a higher level of nitrogen dioxide in your home and this can result in you being more sensitive to triggers than you would otherwise be. One way to reduce this effect is to keep kitchen windows and doors open while you are cooking and to keep doors to the rest of the house shut. If you have severe asthma, it may be worth changing your cooking fuel to another form such as electricity. Gas-fired central heating does not seem to be such a problem as it is vented outside the house.

Carpets and furniture

Some people are sensitive to the formaldehyde gas that is given off by furniture made from medium density fibreboard (MDF). This can be a particular problem when the furniture is new. Carpets can also give off formaldehyde gas. Latex backings to carpets can be a trigger for people with latex allergy. Some people find their asthma gets worse when they have new sofas and chairs and this may be due to the fire-retardant chemicals sprayed on to upholstered

New furniture
The fire-retardant chemicals on new furniture can trigger asthma symptoms.

furniture. If you are sensitive to these things, either avoid them or make sure they are well aired before and after you bring them into the house.

Pets

The allergens produced by furry and feathered pets are particularly hard to get rid of. If you have an allergy to animals, then it is best not to have them in your home at all. If you cannot live without them, make sure that they do not go into your bedroom and main living areas. It is possible to remove pet allergens by steam cleaning, but this is fairly drastic and expensive.

'It took me ages to work out that the new sofa was causing my asthma. I didn't realize it could. Once we'd stuck the sofa in the garden for a week it was miles better.' (Gary, sales representative)

Health

Stress can be a trigger for some people. The best way to deal with an excess of stress in your life is to reduce stressful situations to a minimum and then learn some good relaxation techniques.

Exercise can be very beneficial for asthma sufferers as it improves lung function and aids relaxation. Looking after yourself, eating lots of fresh fruit and vegetables and making sure that you get enough rest and exercise can greatly improve your health and lessen the amount of asthma symptoms you experience.

Flu vaccine
It is advisable for people with asthma to be vaccinated against flu. A new flu vaccine is produced every year to protect against new strains of the virus.

It is best to avoid medicines that can trigger asthma symptoms, especially aspirin and anti-inflammatory drugs. Ask your pharmacist about suitable alternatives.

'Flu's terrible. I had it last year – I was flattened. It got my asthma too. This year I'm going to remember to get my flu jab.' (Ryan, student)

Asthma symptoms are often triggered and made worse by infections, especially virus infections, so vaccinations are important for people with asthma. It is especially important for children with asthma to have their normal childhood vaccinations for diseases such as tetanus, polio, diphtheria, whooping cough, measles, mumps, meningitis and rubella. It is also wise for both adults and children with asthma to have the annual flu vaccine. If you are especially prone to severe chest infections, your doctor may also recommend you have the pneumonia vaccine.

Living with triggers at work or school

If your asthma symptoms are worse at work and improve when you are away from work, you may have occupational asthma. In the European Union, if you are diagnosed with occupational asthma, your employer must protect you from coming into contact with the cause. This may include removing triggers and replacing them with alternatives. For example, if your asthma is triggered by latex and your job involves wearing latex gloves, then your employer

Paint spraying

No one wore masks in the garage for spray jobs. Not real men. The health and safety people tried to make us, but no one wanted to look soft. Then I started having breathing problems after work and got rushed to hospital. I've got asthma now. Stupid really. I wear the mask now – it's either that or stop work. It puts it in perspective. (Carl, paint sprayer)

would be obliged to supply a glove made from a different substance. Alternatively, it may mean installing proper ventilation or, if that does not help, supplying you with breathing equipment to prevent you inhaling the trigger.

If you are sensitive to a substance found at school, for example dust in the woodwork room, fumes from chemistry or metalwork, the fur or feathers of the class pet, you need to let your teacher know. The school nurse or health and safety representative should be able to suggest alternatives to the substance that you are sensitive to, or ways of avoiding it.

Exercise

Exercise is very important for people with asthma as it helps you to become stronger and more resilient to infection and improves your lung function. Exercise can be a trigger for some people with asthma, but this does not mean that you can never exercise; your exercise just needs sensible management.

Some forms of exercise are more likely to provoke asthma than others. Team sports such as netball, football, hockey and rugby can cause

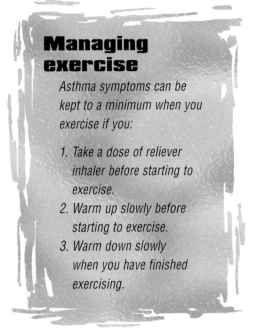

Managing exercise

Asthma symptoms can be kept to a minimum when you exercise if you:

1. *Take a dose of reliever inhaler before starting to exercise.*
2. *Warm up slowly before starting to exercise.*
3. *Warm down slowly when you have finished exercising.*

Tom Dolan

Tom Dolan swam his way into the record books and became an Olympic Gold Medal winner in 1996, despite having asthma.

problems, as they are usually played outside during the winter and cold air and exercise can trigger asthma attacks. This does not mean that you cannot take part in these sports, but you need to be aware of how to minimize your problems. One sensible thing to do is to wear a scarf around your mouth in cold weather, as this helps warm the air before it enters your lungs. It is also important to take your reliever inhaler before going out.

Activities such as yoga and swimming tend to be less risky, although swimmers should beware of cold water and high chlorination, as both can trigger asthma attacks.

Holidays

Holidays can present a problem for people with asthma if the place they are going to increases the likelihood of their coming into contact with a trigger, or if the holiday increases their stress levels. Holidays that can potentially cause a problem include:

- skiing holidays – triggers: cold air, exercise, altitude
- farm holidays – triggers: fur, feathers and pollen
- mountain holidays – triggers: altitude, cold air, exercise
- holidays involving scuba diving – many countries will not allow people with asthma to dive, as the compressed air breathed in by divers, combined with exercise, may trigger an asthma attack, which would be very dangerous underwater.
- activity holidays – exercise-induced asthma.

Before you go away on holidays like these, talk about management techniques with your doctor and work out a plan of what to do if you get into difficulties. Make sure that you carry your inhalers with you at all times.

People with asthma may well find that their symptoms improve on holiday, as they are away from the things that trigger their symptoms at home.

Mountain climbers
People with asthma need to take extra precautions when climbing to high altitudes.

Self-management plans

A self-management plan has two parts, monitoring and treatment. Monitoring your asthma involves taking a peak flow reading morning and evening before you take your inhaler. Peak flow meters measure how hard you can blow air out of your lungs. Measuring your peak flow is important, as you cannot always tell how your lungs are by the way you feel. It also enables you to measure accurately how well your treatment is working.

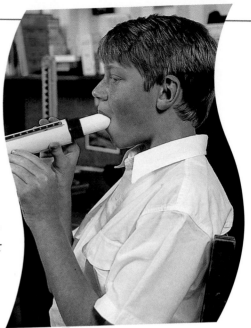

You can then adapt your treatment (following guidelines agreed with your doctor), based on your peak flow readings. For example, your doctor may suggest that, if your peak flow goes down to a certain level, you should increase the amount of preventer you take; or that, if your peak flow reading improves, you may reduce the amount of preventer medication. You may also agree to visit your doctor if your peak flow reading goes below a certain level, or if your symptoms get worse. Self-management plans keep you in control of your asthma and, followed properly, can keep you fitter.

Monitoring peak flow

By measuring your peak flow twice a day, you can stop problems before you feel ill.

Living with asthma does not need to be a problem. It just needs sensible management. Make sure that you go for regular check-ups with your doctor or asthma nurse and regularly review your self-management plan. The better managed your asthma is, the less of a problem it will be. Missing doses or not taking your reliever inhalers when you need to just means that your asthma symptoms will become worse and will cause you more difficulties.

If your asthma gets bad and you need to take time off school, talk to your tutors and work out ways to catch up on the work you have missed. Other people have this problem too; one in seven young people suffers from asthma at some point in their life. You will not be the first person to ask for help, and asking early prevents problems building up later on. Taking medication for asthma can be an issue at school. Children over the age of 7 are usually allowed to carry their own inhalers. It is wise to make sure that a responsible person at the school has a spare inhaler labelled with your name, in case you need it.

'Sometimes I get teased about it. I just ignore them. It's usually only the idiots who haven't got the brains to think of anything else.' (Fran, student)

Some people feel embarrassed about using their inhalers in front of others. They worry that people will tease them, or they may have experienced teasing or bullying about their condition. Either find ways of taking your inhaler discreetly or do it openly with confidence. Often the thing people notice is your feelings of embarrassment. If you do the same thing with confidence, they may not notice it at all. If you are bullied, tell someone. Do not suffer in silence. Whatever you do, do not stop taking your inhalers, as you could end up ill and in a worse state than before.

It is possible to live a normal life if you have asthma. When asthma is well managed and under control, few people will be aware that you have it and you can get on and live life to the full.

Going for gold
You can live a normal life when you have asthma – joining in and aiming high !

Glossary

adrenalin   a naturally occurring hormone that helps your body to respond to stressful situations. It is used as a medicine to combat the effects of a severe allergic reaction.

allergen   a substance that causes an allergy.

allergy   a problem that occurs when your immune system reacts to a harmless substance as if it were a dangerous virus, bacteria or parasite.

anaphylaxis   a severe form of allergic reaction.

antibodies   substances produced by the immune system that roam around your body neutralizing bacteria and viruses.

antihistamine   a medicine used to treat the effects of a mild to moderate allergic reaction.

bacteria   minute, single-cell organisms that can cause disease.

bronchitis   an illness where your bronchioles become inflamed and you develop a cough.

carbon dioxide   a colourless gas that is a waste product from energy production in your body. It is removed from your body through your lungs when you breathe out.

damp dusting   an efficient method of dusting, using a slightly dampened cloth. The moisture on the cloth traps the dust and prevents it from flying into the air.

desensitization   a method of reducing your body's sensitivity to a substance, and so reducing the severity of an allergy.

diagnosis   the doctor's expert opinion about the name of the disease that is causing your problems.

expiration   breathing out.

faeces   solid waste excreted from the digestive tract (poo or droppings).

fire-retardant chemicals   chemicals that do not burn easily. They are often sprayed onto soft furnishings in order to reduce the likelihood of their bursting into flame if, for example, cigarette ash is dropped on them.

genes   parts of the genetic code present in each of your body cells and controlling how your body grows and develops. You inherit your genetic code from your parents and pass it on to your children.

genetically inherited   passed on by parents through their genes. Characteristics such as eye and hair colour and even whether we tend to have a short temper are passed on in this way.

hay fever   an allergic condition where pollen irritates the lining of your nose and causes sneezing and mucus production.

histamine   a chemical released in response to infection, allergy or injury, which results in inflammation.

homeopathy   an alternative therapy where the person is treated by being given tiny amounts of a substance that, in larger doses, would produce similar symptoms to those he or she is suffering.

IgE   immunoglobulin E, the antibody involved in allergies.

immune system	the body's defence system. It searches out and destroys viruses and bacteria, protecting you from infection.
inhaler	a gadget that produces a fine mist of medicine, which the user breathes in.
inspiration	breathing in.
intravenous	given straight into the blood supply through a small needle inserted into a vein, usually in the arm.
menopause	the time during which a woman's periods gradually stop.
menstrual cycle	the monthly reproductive cycle in women, involving egg release, preparation of the lining of the uterus for an embryo, and discharge of that lining (known as menstruation or a period).
mucus	fluid produced by the lungs and other mucous membranes in the body. In your lungs, mucus is used to trap foreign bodies and particles of dust, to stop them irritating your airways. In healthy lungs, the mucus is clear. If you have a chest infection, it can become thick or runny, green or yellow.
nebulizer	a piece of equipment supplied with inhaler medicine that produces a mist. It is used to deliver medicine to your lungs.
non-steroidal anti-inflammatory drugs	medicines that reduce inflammation and do not contain steroids.
osteoporosis	a condition where bones become very brittle and fragile due to calcium loss.
oxygen	a colourless gas present in the air around us, which is absorbed into our bloodstream when we breathe in. It is used to produce energy in our body cells.
parasite	any organism that lives in or on another organism. In humans, these include tapeworms, threadworms and headlice.
perennial rhinitis	an allergic condition causing sneezing and a runny nose.
prescribed	recommended by a doctor.
reproductive system	the parts of your body involved in reproduction.
respiratory tract	the airways through which air passes on its way to and through your lungs.
saliva	fluid produced in your mouth that helps you to swallow your food and starts to digest it.
spacer	a gadget used to help you get the best from your inhaler. It makes it easier to inhale the correct dose of medicine.
steroids	a group of drugs that mimic the action of the body's natural steroids – hormones. They are often used to reduce inflammation and swelling.
virus	an infective agent that, once it gets inside a cell, reproduces and rapidly infects other cells. Viruses are responsible for many illnesses, including the common cold, flu, chickenpox and herpes.

Resources

Organizations in the UK

National Asthma Campaign
Providence House,
Providence Place,
London N1 0NT

Telephone 0207 226 2260

This is an independent charity which works with people with asthma to overcome the disease. It funds a great deal of research into asthma and offers education and support. It provides many resources for people interested in asthma, including fact sheets, booklets and magazines. It also provides information packs for schools.

Asthma Help Line: 0845 701 0203
This help line run by the National Asthma Campaign is open Monday to Friday, 9 am-7 pm.

Global Initiative for Asthma
GINA secretariat,
Montpellier,
France

This is an organization made up of a collaboration between the National Heart, Lung and Blood Institute and the World Health Organization. It also supervises and coordinates activities for World Asthma Day. It has information about World Asthma Day and publishes research findings.

British Lung Foundation
78 Hatton Gardens,
London EC1N 8LD

This British charity funds research into the prevention, diagnosis, treatment and cure of all lung diseases. It publishes some very useful fact sheets and booklets.

Organizations in the USA

The American Lung Association®
61 Broadway, 6th Floor
NY 10006

This American research and education foundation has useful information about all lung diseases. It has many local centres around the USA.

Asthma and Allergy Foundation of America (AAFA)
Southern CA Chapter
5900 Wilshire Boulevard
2330 Los Angeles
CA. 90036

Lots of research and information about all aspects of allergy and asthma.

Films

Bad Behaviour, 1993, staring Stephen Rea, Sinead Cusack, Phillip Jackson and Clair Higgins. Director: Les Blair.
This is a humorous film about the life of an everyday family. The main character, played by Stephen Rea, has asthma, which he copes with very well.

Sidekicks, 1993, staring Beau Bridges, Chuck Norris, and Jonathan Brandis. Director: Aaron Norris.
This is a story about a boy who has severe asthma and survives by living in a dream world. He is bullied at school about his asthma and takes up karate lessons in order to defend himself.

Index

acupuncture 48
adrenalin 20
air filters 53
air pollution 16, 24, 27, 28,
     29, 31, 37
airways 4, 6, 7, 8, 9, 10, 11,
     14, 15, 16, 19, 23, 24, 31,
     34, 36, 37, 39, 40, 41, 42,
     43, 44
allergens 19, 20, 21, 22, 28,
     29, 30, 33, 35, 37, 41, 45,
     54
allergies 16, 17, 18, 19, 20,
     21, 22, 23, 27, 28, 29, 30,
     34, 37, 41, 45, 49, 53, 54
allergy-related asthma 15,
     17, 21, 22, 29, 30, 33, 45,
     46
allergy-related illness 13, 29,
     30
allergy tests 22, 26
altitude 57
alveolar surface 9
alveoli 8, 9, 10
anaphylaxis 20, 46
animals 18, 21, 34, 54
antibiotics 45, 47
antibodies 15, 17, 19, 22, 37
antihistamines 17, 46
antileukotrines 40, 42
aspirin 24, 35, 55
asthma nurse 15, 38, 39, 42,
     58
asthma organizations 26
atopy 17
Australia 4, 26

babies 19, 30, 33
bacteria 17, 18, 19, 35, 45
barbecues 24
bee stings 20
beta-blockers 24, 36
blood tests 15, 22
breast-feeding 30
breathing 6, 7, 8, 9, 10, 11,
     12, 14, 24, 38, 39, 42
breathing exercises 47, 49
breathlessness 4, 10, 11, 13
bronchi 8, 9
bronchiole 8, 9
bronchitis 28
bronchoprovocation 14

capillaries 9
carbon dioxide 6, 7, 9
cars 27, 28, 37
cats 21
cells 6, 7
chemicals 16, 23, 24, 25, 28,
     32, 34, 53
cigarette smoke 16, 23, 24,
     27, 32, 33, 52
cleaners 25, 32, 34, 35
cleanliness 18, 34
cold air 31, 57
cold (virus) 11, 23, 36
complementary therapies 47-9
coughing 8, 11, 13, 15, 36

damp dusting 51, 53
death from asthma 5, 11, 29
desensitization 16, 45, 46
diagnosis 13-15

diesel engines 28, 37
diving 57
dogs 16, 21
Dolan, Tom 56
dust 32, 56

eczema 13, 17, 20
electronics industry 32
emotion 16, 23
energy 6, 7, 11
environments 5, 13, 17, 18,
     37
exercise 11, 13, 16, 23, 54,
     56, 57
exercise-based therapies 47,
     48

flu 23, 36, 54, 55
flu vaccine 54, 55
food additives 21
foods 21
furniture 53

gas cookers and heaters 24,
     34, 53
genes, genetic susceptibility to
     asthma 5, 13, 17, 24, 26,
     28, 30, 37
genetic engineering 29
Global Strategy for Asthma
     26, 27
growth 11, 41, 44

hay fever 13, 17, 19, 20, 21
histamine 19, 20, 41, 46
holidays 57

homeopathy 49
homes 31, 33, 34, 35, 37, 51, 52, 53, 54, 57
hormones 16, 23, 25
hospital treatment 46, 47
house dust mites 18, 20, 21, 33, 34, 37, 50, 51

immune system 11, 17, 18, 19, 30, 35, 36, 41, 45, 46
immunoglobulin E (IgE) 15, 17, 19, 22
incidence of asthma 4, 26, 27, 33
industrial pollution 27, 37
inhalers 5, 12, 15, 16, 21, 38, 39, 40, 42, 43, 56, 57, 58, 59
isocyanates 32

Japan 28

larynx 7, 8, 9
latex 20, 31, 32, 53, 55-6
Leipzig 27, 28
leukotrines 42
lungs 4, 6, 7, 8, 9, 11, 14, 28, 29, 40, 42, 43, 56, 57, 58

massage 48
mast cells 19, 20, 41
mast cell stabilizers 40, 41
medicines (asthma triggers) 16, 23, 24, 35, 36, 55
medicines for asthma 11, 12, 38, 39, 40, 41, 42, 43, 44, 46, 47
medicines, herbal 48, 49
meditation 48
menopause 25

moulds 18, 20, 21, 30, 31
mould spores 15, 21, 30, 31
mouth 7, 8, 41
mucus 8, 11, 37
Munich 27, 28

nebulizer 15, 43, 46, 47
New Zealand 4, 26
night 11, 13, 15
nose 7, 8, 29

occupational asthma 25, 31, 32, 55
oil-seed rape 29
oxygen 6, 7, 9, 10, 11, 15, 23, 47

paints 25, 55
parasites 17, 19, 35
peak flow tests 14, 58
perennial rhinitis 20, 21, 30
perfumes 25
pets 19, 20, 34, 54, 56
pharynx 7, 8
pneumonia vaccine 55
pollen 18, 19, 20, 21, 29, 30, 31, 46, 52, 53, 57
pollen count 53
pregnancy 25, 33, 37
preventers 38, 39, 40, 58

relaxation 48, 49, 54
relievers 38, 39, 43, 46, 47, 56, 57, 58
respiratory tract 7, 8, 9
reversibility of asthma 4, 11

school 56, 58, 59
self-management plan 12, 58
skin prick tests 22, 45

smoke 24
smoking 37, 52 (*see also* cigarette smoke)
sneezing 7, 17, 29, 36
solvents 25
spacer 12, 41, 43
spinhaler 40
spirometry 14
sports 56, 57
steroids, inhaled 40, 41, 43
steroid tablets 12, 15, 44, 47
stress 16, 23, 48, 54, 57
swimming 56, 57
symptoms 13, 38, 39, 41, 47, 50, 51, 54, 55, 56, 58

t'ai chi 47
thunderstorms 25, 31
trachea 8
traffic 24
triggers 4, 5, 15, 16, 28, 31, 32, 34, 38, 39, 40, 50, 51, 52, 53, 54, 55, 56, 57

urban environment 27-9

vaccinations 54, 55
vacuum cleaning 50, 51, 52, 53
viruses 17, 19, 35, 36, 37
virus infections 11, 16, 23, 24, 36, 37, 44, 45, 46, 55

weather 16, 23, 25, 31
wheezing 4, 10, 13, 14, 16, 20, 21, 23, 37
workplace 31-2, 55
World Asthma Day 26

yoga 47, 49, 57